The Character of Leadership
An Ancient Model for a Quantum Age

The Character of Leadership
An Ancient Model for a Quantum Age

Philip H. Eastman II

Leadership Advisors, Inc.
Boise

Leadership Advisors, Inc.
2214 Tawny Woods Place
Boise, ID 83706

www.characterofleadership.com

An exhaustive search was done to determine whether previously published material included in this book required permission to reprint. If there has been an error, a correction will be made on subsequent editions.

Man's Search for Meaning by Viktor E. Frankl
Copyright © 1959, 1962, 1984, 1992 by Viktor E. Frankl
Restated by permission of Beacon Press, Boston

Churchill's quotations: Reproduced with permission of Curtis Brown Ltd, London on behalf of The Estate of Winston Churchill - Copyright © Winston S. Churchill

Webster's New International Dictionary. 2nd ed. 1934

Publishers Cataloging-in-Publication Data

Eastman, Philip H., 1960-
The character of leadership: an ancient model for a quantum age/by Philip H. Eastman II

   p. cm.

   ISBN: 978-0-615-28987-8

   Includes bibliographical references.

   1. Leadership. 2. Leadership – Moral and ethical aspects. 3. Character.
   Business ethics. I. Title.

   HD 57.7.E238
   658.4092-dc22
   2009927189

Published in Boise, Idaho by Leadership Advisors, Inc.

Design and Layout by Mike Schroeder

Printed in the United States of America

J   I   H   G   F   E   D   C   B   A

Acknowledgments

I am grateful to many who helped bring to fruition the book you are holding. I especially want to acknowledge the many leaders whose experiences provide illustrations for the character of leadership.

Thank you to my business partner Lorene Rasmussen for her vision and tenacious dedication to bringing this work to you. Her commitment to this work exemplifies hope and courage.

Thanks also to:
- Kevin Booe, for teaching Lorene how to read a copyright page and his insights on nonfiction work.
- Sylvia Marmon, for her initial editing when many of these chapters were articles.
- Karl Meinhardt, for listening to me, setting up the website, and for asking the tough questions.
- Cynthia Tank, for editing, proofreading, and challenging my concepts.
- Marilyn Taylor, for help with the copyright page and subject tracing.
- Mike Schroeder, for his extraordinary ability to take my words and turn them into cover art.
- Thanks to those who took the time to read different iterations, provide constructive feedback, and lend their names through endorsement to this work.
- Our clients, who embrace and live out the character model in their daily lives.

I am thankful to my parents, Ruth and Phil Eastman, for their profound influence and wisdom in my life.

Most importantly, I thank my wife of twenty-five years, Connie Eastman, for epitomizing love and for her unfailing commitment to me.

Finally, for our sons, Philip and Keith, I thank you both for being men of faith.

What Leaders are saying:

"I've had the good fortune of working with Phil Eastman for several years. I know him to be an absolute authority on 'Change Management' - how change effects people and organizations, how to manage through those changes, and how to come out the other side as quickly and efficiently as possible. Now he is tackling 'Leadership' in the same straight-forward fashion. You will find this a quick read and come away with valuable, real world ideas on how to apply these to your personal and professional lives."

~ Garry Beaty, CIO - City of Boise

"Many books have been written about great leaders and leadership qualities, but the Character of Leadership goes even deeper. Phil explores leadership in a refreshing, almost spiritual way to bring us full circle toward understanding the essence of authentic leadership through a character model. It's a leadership study complete with historical and personal examples, including guidelines for modeling behaviors at each stage. Perhaps today, more than ever, we need leaders who embody Phil's character model of leadership."

~ Terri Hughes, Director of Organizational Change – Supervalu

"In our current 7/24, hectic, busy world, leaders are turning more and more to basic foundational truths for guidance and direction for their organizations. Phil Eastman, in The Character of Leadership, provides a clear and concise roadmap of these truths. The Character of Leadership is a must read for any leader seeking the next level in their organization, regardless of the type."

~ Peter J. Oliver, Partner – Brighton Corporation

"Vince Lombardi reminded us that, "Great leaders are made, they are not born." Phil gives sound, age-old wisdom through seven virtue-centered elements that helps define leadership character. They are inextricably related and the nexus among them is undeniable. Quality leadership starts from the inside-out. If we don't possess these core virtues personally, chances are we won't develop them managerially or organizationally to become effective, successful leaders. The more we live and model these virtues in our professional duties, the greater the likelihood others with whom we work will adopt them as well. The Character of Leadership is a must read for everyone to self examine our personal belief system foundation so that we continually develop leadership behaviors for ourselves and others."

~ Mike Masterson, Chief of Police – City of Boise

"What a great read! I firmly believe the common 'chink in the armor' of most organizations is the lack of providing true development for their leaders. Phil candidly addresses the critical topic of leadership in this book, and brings some insights into focus that should literally turn the classic org chart structure upside-down!"

~ Peter Mannos, Director of Retail Development - Brooks Sports

"*The Character of Leadership* prescribes the antidote for today's "what's in it for me" leadership culture. You will be compelled to action by Phil Eastman's straightforward style and incisive wisdom."

~ Tony Greer, Plant Manager – R.C. Bigelow Inc.

"This book will frustrate those looking for a leadership quick tip. Those books abound. But for the leadership student, this book will be a refreshing read. I have known Phil Eastman for a number of years and have seen him model the principles described. Enjoy the book and enjoy the opportunity to be a leader that can make a real difference."

~ Dwight Pond, Senior Director, IT - Supervalu

"In his book, *The Character of Leadership: An Ancient Model for a Quantum Age*, Phil Eastman concisely describes the seven elements he believes are key to leadership. At the end of each chapter, he presents specific leadership behaviors that demonstrate the particular component of the model – allowing the reader to do some self-reflection. This is a must read for anyone who is in a position of leadership."

~ Sheri Coleman, Curriculum Director - Hot Springs, South Dakota School District

"This book is brief, but very thought provoking so that it takes a lot of time to read properly. Each chapter adds components with observations that induce the reader to pause and reflect. The net effect is that the model comes together in a profound manner. If the reader takes the time to reflect as he or she reads, the message is powerful."

~ Kenneth A. Smith, PhD, CPA - Dean of the College of Business and Professor of Accounting, Idaho State University

"Phil Eastman's volume focuses the topic of leadership exactly where it ought to be-on the personal character of the leader. Using compelling examples from history and illustrations from his own years of experience, Eastman leads the reader through seven classic character traits essential for successful leadership. This is a book that should be read by all those who aspire to lead."

~ Mark L. Strauss, Ph.D.- Professor of New Testament, Bethel Seminary San Diego

"Leadership reflects many characteristics of both the leader and the situation; but above all, it is driven by the character of the leader. This volume highlights this most important dimension of the leadership journey with clarity, vision and passion. A must read for all involved with or care about quality leadership."

~ Charles Ruch, Ph.D. - President Emeritus, South Dakota School of Mines.

Letter from the Author

In January 2007, my business partner Lorene Rasmussen announced her intention to run the Marine Corps Marathon, a race she had always wanted to run but had never taken the time to train or prepare for. She joined a running club and learned the basic principles of endurance running in order to finish 26.2 miles.

After 12 grueling months of training, shin splints, fueling and hydrating, multiple short races, and hundreds of miles of running, Lorene finished her first marathon. We were all so proud of her!

Now to be sure, I'm no marathoner, but I was encouraged and challenged by her example to undertake my own marathon of sorts, one that has been before me since the founding of Leadership Advisors Group in 1998: the very book you are holding in your hands today.

As if the sheer discipline it takes to write a book wasn't enough to deter me, I also felt constrained by a few misconceptions, the first being that everything that needs to be said or written on leadership has already been said and written. Misconception number two was that if there was something new to be said about leadership, I was certainly not the one to say it. And lastly, like Lorene, I never thought I would have the time to take on such a marathon of a project.

Recognizing those misconceptions for what they were, I finally announced my intentions to write this book, and with the support of family, friends, fellow business leaders—and the well-meaning pestering of my business partner—the manuscript went to print.

"Leadership" is a broad topic, situational in application and organic in nature. I won't pretend to think this will be the final word on the matter. I do, however, believe that the model you are about to become familiar with is a strong framework that will withstand the weight of future conversations.

We all know by now that the government cannot make enough laws to correct the problems we continue to face in the 21st century. The reason? These are not legal problems; they are character problems. As such, they need to be addressed by leaders courageous enough to live an examined life, because leadership is an inside-out proposition.

Socrates was noted for saying, "the unexamined life is a life not worth living." Today we refer to this as being self-aware, or understanding what motivates our own behavior.

During Plato's time, Greek thinkers had already established the idea that a good person possessed four cardinal virtues: courage, temperance, justice, and wisdom. After the time of Christ, the church fathers added three more: faith, hope, and love. Living these seven virtues together was considered to be a life of "habitual excellence."

Likewise, the Character of Leadership Model has seven elements. They are distinctive in nature yet interrelated, with faith as the central element. As you become familiar with the other elements that radiate from faith, you will begin to understand how this ancient model can be applied today in order for leaders to successfully catapult us into the future.

Thank you for joining us.

[handwritten margin notes:]

Greek cardinal Virtues:
Courage
Temperance
Wisdom
Justice
Faith
Hope
Love

Church IX 3mrs

Contents

Chapter One

Character & Leadership in a Quantum Age

"Leadership is an inside-out proposition."

Gregory W Bourgond

Leadership is not merely a matter of understanding what behaviors to employ. It's also a matter of character. I first came across this powerful insight into leadership while working on my master's degree in theological studies. I began my master's work in 1999 just one year after leaving the bank where I had been an executive. The pursuit of a seminary degree had long been a goal of mine. I wanted to understand more about the spiritual nature of human beings. That, combined with a strong curiosity in history, led me to Bethel Seminary. Over five years I would take numerous classes that would reinforce many of my understandings and challenge many others. Dr. Greg Bourgond taught one of my first courses, and in his opening lecture he planted a seed that would eventually lead to this writing. In a simple and matter-of-fact voice he said, "Leadership is an inside-out proposition." As powerful as that insight was, it did not answer the deeper question: What is character?

In the process of exploring the subject of character and leadership, I came across a short dictionary entry that defined character according to seven essential components or, as the ancients called them, virtues: Faith, Courage, Wisdom, Temperance, Hope, Justice, and Love. That was the moment the trajectory for this book was born. I knew that this model represented an important step in the understanding and application of character as a paradigm for leadership.

Virtues

The idea that character was important was certainly not news to me. Like most people, I grew up hearing the steady mantra that character matters. But it was the late 1960s, and the rules of acceptable behavior were morphing almost daily. As a teenager in the 1970s, I saw the ramifications of the excessive behaviors of the '60s: the disgrace of a presidential resignation, corruption on a national scale, capitalism's resurgence, unbridled greed, and the overarching worship of individualism.

The backdrop of the '60s and the abandonment of social mores left me somewhat emptied of the moral tools that my parents' generation took for granted. The adults whose characters were shaped against the background of the Great Depression were part of a time when interdependence required cultural values that were widely held and routinely followed. I wanted to understand their simple, shared definition of character but needed to mix with it an appreciation of the range of individual expressions of character. That pursuit added to my keen desire to understand the ties between character and leadership, how to lead people in ways they deserve to be led and to enable others to do the same. If the proposition that leadership is inside out is correct then the understanding of what is *inside* the leader is of paramount concern.

This, however, raises one more question: Can one's character—and the leadership that flows from that character—be shaped, or is character a fixed quality in the individual? Well, I am not a psychologist, nor do I profess to have some singular insight into the human psyche; that sort of insight would require more than several lifetimes of experience. I have, however, seen in myself and others the ability to make meaningful, profound, and positive changes, not just in leadership behavior, but also in the very nature of who we are. Our character is shaped and refined by success, setbacks, and the painful experience of failure. As a consequence, some of us choose to make a transformation in our character that forever alters the way we see life, people, work, and our leadership responsibilities.

So, can character and the leadership that flows from it be purposely shaped? Absolutely! However, there is no pain-free way to develop character. It is much like that inevitable diet after the holidays. Nothing known to dieters will help us lose those unwanted pounds except the discipline of eating less and moving more. Character development has the same reality.

All human development is a function of self-awareness, practice, and refinement. So developing the character that gives rise to leadership requires embracing a realistic model of character, determining where your character stands relative to that model, and then adopting the leadership behaviors associated with that model.

The Challenge

*Model
Standing
adoption*

4

[Handwritten margin note, top:] 7 Virtues of character
Justice   Faith
Courage   Hope
Wisdom   Love
Temperance

To articulate the character model and define its seven elements, we need to turn to people who spent their lives considering this complex subject. Aristotle and his contemporaries determined that character was made up of four virtues: Justice, Courage, Wisdom, and Temperance.

These four virtues explained the essence of a person. That ancient philosopher's model was supplemented 2000 years ago by the arrival on the world scene of a new branch of Judaism that would eventually blossom into Christianity. The "people of the way," as the early followers of Jesus were called, understood the power that ancient Greek philosophy had over the minds of people of their day. They also understood that a frontal attack on Greek philosophy using the tenets of the blossoming Christian movement would likely repulse potential followers. Instead, the apologists simply augmented the fourfold model with three additional virtues that more fully described human character and that recognized the essential fact that people are multi-faceted beings. The "people of the way" added Faith, Hope, and Love to the list of virtues to round out what has come to be understood as the seven virtues of character.

[Handwritten margin notes, right:] Aristotle — Four Virtues — Justice, Courage, Wisdom, Temperance — People of the Way — Faith, Hope, Love

Interactions of the elements

Although we will use the ancients' list of virtues (we will call them elements), it is the interaction of the elements that accounts for the synergistic complexity of our model. Consider the graphic representation of the character model, a model that offers us distinct advantages or liberties of interpretation.

3-D

Our first liberty is to view character as a three-dimensional object rather than just an abstract mental model. Of course, the intricacies of personal character cannot adequately be depicted graphically, but for the sake of understanding, take a look at the adjoining illustration. If character were an object, it would be a sphere with a core at its center. One of the character elements is at the core with the six remaining elements linked one to another and connected to the core. Our goal with this depiction is twofold: first, to see character as something real that can be managed, molded, and changed. At the same time we want to depict the complex nature of character and how one element affects the others.

Interaction

Justice
Courage
Temperance
Faith
Love
Hope
Wisdom

To this end, we have shown the elements connected to each other like pieces of a puzzle. The mechanical fasteners demonstrate the interconnectedness of each element to the others, but please realize that the connection of the elements is more organic than mechanical. The reality of their interplay remains a miracle and mystery of our humanity.

Our second liberty has to do with placing Faith as the core element of the model. The ancients did not contemplate this view of character, but in my experience Faith is the element that inevitably gives rise to how the rest of the elements play out.

Faith

We describe the model as being three-dimensional to show that while the elements are singular, they function in relation to one another to comprise human character.

3-D

Having this three-dimensional illustration is helpful, but in reality there is another more challenging facet of the character of leadership: the demonstration and observation of leadership behaviors in relation to a specific environment.

Environment

Conceiving the ancients' model as dimensional has important implications. I mentioned that the genesis of this book came from my experience while obtaining my master's degree. Studying ancient texts was both challenging and exhilarating, but the most important lesson from five years in seminary was this: Context is everything! It would be wrong to present our model and not address the quantum realities in which this model is applied.

Context

In our use of the word "quantum," we are asserting the following:

Quantum

- The leadership arising from the leader's character is connected to the context in which it is observed. The leader is an intimate part of a human system that she is both responsible for and accountable to.

- The behaviors must adjust based on the circumstances and relationships in which the leader is operating.

- These behaviors shift even as they are observed by others engaged in the same system.

This systematic way of thinking takes us away from those formulaic approaches to leadership—euphemistically called "best practices"—that produce robotic patterns in leaders.

Best Practices

Responsibility Account

8

Living in a quantum age means ours is a time in which the discoveries of science have not changed the world but rather expanded what we know about the physical environment in which we operate. The application of those expanding concepts of quantum physics and chaos theory to organizations has both destabilized and liberated leaders.

The destabilization comes when the rules and tools of the past no longer seem to have the same effect. Perhaps one of the most telling examples of this is the command-and-control oriented leader who still possesses the authority of leadership but finds that the followers do not respond to orders alone—they must be convinced to follow.

The discomfort of destabilization, however, is more than offset by the realization that today's complex organizations have infinitely more potential for achievement than their predecessors. In today's organization, leaders are liberated from outdated constructs and required to engage in new ways. A common and simple manifestation of the freedom to lead comes when organizations employ cross-functional teams to solve problems, take advantage of opportunities, or

What Potential are you missing?

improve processes. Crossing organizational boundaries requires a different kind of leadership than does command-and–control, and that leadership is best built on a foundation of character.

Bridge

Our model serves as the bridge between old truths of character and the leadership needed in today's highly complex operating context. However, there are many types of bridges. Some are massive structures built to cross chasms and requiring enormous structural supports, fixed against the forces that batter them. Another type of bridge uses large buoyant containers, pontoons, floating on the water to sustain the driving surface. Floating bridges rise and fall with the water levels, adjust to the winds, and allow boats to pass, all the while providing a stable means for movement.

Our model is a floating bridge between the ancients' view of character and our own quantum age. It provides a flexible, resilient way to move past the challenges and opportunities leaders face. It is flexible enough to move with the changing conditions, meaning that you will need to tailor it to fit your setting. However, it is resilient enough to be invaluable in any organization. We encourage you to trust the strength of the model for your leadership.

The 7 Virtues of Character

Chapter Two

Faith

*" . . . to achieve a frame of mind in which
I may hold firmly to what I believe to
be true, even though I know that it
might conceivably be false."*
Michael Polanyi

For a number of years in the United States there has been
hesitancy to discuss faith in government, business, and
nonprofit settings. In presentations featuring our character
model, a palpable tension sweeps over the room as listeners
realize that the first element of discussion will be Faith. The
nervousness may arise from the view that somehow there
are certain domains in which discussions of Faith are
appropriate, while in other settings the topic is and should
remain off-limits.

However, there is no way to have a discussion about
human behavior and character without discussing Faith and
the beliefs it harbors. Discussing this touchy but critical
element of character will illuminate the clear connection
between Faith and the nature and quality of leadership.

As noted earlier, the graphic we use to illustrate the elements of character and their interconnectivity shows Faith at the center. Faith is central to character and thus central to leadership behavior that flows from character. The rest of the character elements take their cue from the individual beliefs contained in Faith. Those beliefs inform, color, and influence the rest of the elements in ways that many may not be able to discern except through a clear-eyed, open-minded review of character.

Since Faith is central to our character and to our analysis of leadership, let's dissect this touchy matter, beginning with why Faith is so important.

Believing Is Seeing

People do not act on what they know; they act on what they believe. This simple and troublesome truth makes people marvelous, adaptable, and frustrating. If changing human behavior were as simple as imparting new knowledge, the world would be full of highly educated, successful people living in peace and harmony with each other and their surroundings. Poverty, wars, and environmental degradation occur not because we lack the knowledge upon which to avoid or solve these protracted problems, but because our core beliefs don't accommodate or desire the solutions to be put in place.

For example, let's look at a period in history that saw the rise of labor unions in meaningful and powerful ways in the United States. The Industrial Age brought with it substantial improvements in the efficiency of machines and manufacturing systems. The creation of broad wealth domestically and abroad increased demands for American goods, and the industrialists of the day took full advantage of the opportunity. They worked both adults and children in sweat shops and boiler rooms, in intolerable conditions for countless hours, at low wages—all for the sake of creating for themselves the substantial wealth they *believed* they were entitled to.

There was also a persistent belief among those early industrialists that they were somehow superior to those they employed. There was a distinct class structure that kept the workers in their place, while the families of the entitled few would luxuriate in the efforts of the masses.

These intolerable conditions grew to be more than workers could take physically, emotionally, and economically, so they banded together to create for themselves power that rivaled that of the company owners. In doing so, they perfected the U.S. labor movement, which sought to bring a balance of power to the relationship between workers and companies.

Of course, because these core beliefs about the classes of society were firmly in place as the unions grew, the leaders of those organizations grew more powerful and wealthy. In fact, in some situations they even took advantage of the very workers they were supposed to represent.

The point of this example is that the prevailing belief during that period in history was this: Some people were more valuable than others, even though the U.S. Constitution promises that all are created equal. Wealth and power were something to be accumulated at all cost, whether by industrialist or labor union boss.

Even today, despite legislation and the almost universal acknowledgement that all human beings have the right to be respected, we still use money and power to shape individuals and nations alike. Our knowledge of what is right is superseded by our belief in our own superiority and supremacy. Consequently, we believe we deserve everything we can accumulate.

Let's look at this example from a leadership perspective. I worked in the corporate banking arena for seventeen years, making loans to and collecting loans from businesses large and small. My training was intense and mostly on the job.

Being a good corporate banker requires keen judgment. Banks operate on very thin margins and as a result must collect nearly 100% of the principal they lend, along with interest, in order to remain profitable. Hence, I was trained to be conservative about who received loans and aggressive in collecting the bank's money so we could prosper as an organization.

As a result of my conservative indoctrination, I adopted some fundamental beliefs. One was that people will try to get away with things; therefore, they must be watched to make sure they don't take advantage of the bank. I also believed I needed to control the decisions of the bank since I was uniquely trained and qualified to make the best judgments as to a client's credit worthiness. Together these two beliefs created in me a skepticism of many things and people. That skepticism ate at my soul; I'm still not proud of the ways in which it manifested itself.

In 1998, I happily left banking behind but did not leave behind those two beliefs. Then I met Ron Jenson, who questioned my fundamental beliefs about people and my definition of good judgment.

Ron, an author, friend, and mentor, challenged me to believe the best about people, to lose my skepticism and cynical attitude. He encouraged me to understand that, counter to my views at the time, people are smart and they try to do the right thing. As I began to see people through a new lens, I was relieved to see that Ron was correct. In fact, I already had examples in my own life that validated this realistic and more progressive view of people.

Today, I truly believe the best about people, and this colors my attitudes toward them. That, in turn, substantially informs my approach to leadership development and coaching. It is important to recognize that not everyone fits into this rosy-colored view of humanity. But, to turn a familiar phrase, "seeing is believing" could actually be "believing is seeing."

My story illustrates a very important and encouraging aspect of Faith: It is a dynamic and conscious process, not static and immutable. Human beings have an incredible ability to shift their beliefs about the world and its people at will (although not quickly). This dynamism is integral to our understanding and acceptance of others. The fact that belief is a conscious process frightens many of us. Our initial belief structure comes to us as children and we willingly accept what others tell us about the world. The real power of our humanity comes as we mature and realize that belief is a conscious act, that we don't have to inherit our beliefs; we can choose them. This power is critical to the establishment of the Faith that is central to our model.

Faith Defined

Webster's Dictionary defines Faith as "the disposition to accept as real, true or the like, that which is not supported by sensible evidence or rational proofs."

Faith is the element we humans use to answer our most intimate and important questions—about ourselves, the world we live in, and the people with whom we choose to interact.

Faith is the element of our character in which we store a myriad of core beliefs that answer three universal questions:

- Where did I come from?
- Where am I going?
- How do I matter while I am here?

Let me be clear about this aspect of Faith. In the context of leadership, it is not synonymous with religious expression or a spiritual devotion. Faith as an element of human character is religiously neutral. However, religious teachings—the means people use to engage their religious expression—are contained in a person's faith. Every person has faith but not every one expresses that faith through spirituality. Individuals may place their faith in many other things, such as people, family, money, abilities, government, institutions, and the like. Regardless of a person's spiritual leanings or lack thereof, *it is faith that ignites and empowers belief.*

My purpose is not to advocate where you put your Faith. My purpose is to advocate that you make a conscious choice about where you put your Faith. One of the great wastes of individual capability is the failure to consider the objects, beings, and actions in which we place our Faith.

Belief Motivates Behavior

The second major reason for placing Faith at the center of the character model is to recognize that people behave based on what they believe, not on what they know. This is why changing behavior is such a challenge.

Consider this from a leadership development standpoint. Most of us have been to countless training sessions where the facilitator presents some interesting and often very useful concepts and techniques to help the participants improve their leadership capabilities. However, none of these tips, techniques, or behavior changes has any lasting effect without an accompanying change in belief.

In our leadership development work we know that our efforts will produce the most fruit for a leader when he or she is highly motivated to change. This motivation can be either positive or negative but, alas, many times in our work it is the pain of failure or the fear of inadequacy that motivates a change in belief. But this motivation means that the training will result in true leadership transformation, not just short-term behavior modification.

We believe Faith is fundamental to how our character is displayed in leadership. We also believe that Faith is fundamental to how we interpret and express the other elements of character. In other words, what I understand about Justice or Hope is inextricably linked to where I place my Faith and how I answer those three universal questions: —————————————————————————

- Where did I come from?
- Where am I going?
- How do I matter while I am here?

If my answers to these questions are:

- I don't know
- I don't care
- By making the most money possible

I will have a vastly different approach to justice for myself and others than if I answer the questions this way:

- I came from God
- I am returning to God
- By making a difference in the lives of people

To illustrate this, let me offer the stunning contrast between two historic leaders: Joseph Stalin and Mohandas Gandhi. Joseph Stalin was the undisputed dictatorial leader of the former Soviet Union after the death of its intellectual creator Vladimir Lenin in 1924. From the time Stalin took over leadership of the Communist Party he began a systematic reign of terror. He built an industrial complex, centralized the production of food, crushed Hitler's German army, carved out much of central Europe and all of Eastern Europe for Soviet domination, and in the course of his reign indiscriminately executed or starved six million of his fellow countrymen. Stalin's beliefs about life and people were evident in his speeches and writings, none of which more clearly captured his belief than this one: "Death is the solution to all problems. No man—no problem."

His hard-line brutality was known during his tenure and has become even more evident as the secrecy of his regime has dropped away. Stalin was willing to brutalize and murder anyone who stepped in the way of his lusts. He put his Faith in power and control, and thus his leadership demonstrated those beliefs to the extreme.

Contrast Stalin with Mohandas K. Gandhi (often referred to as Mahatma, meaning "great soul"). Gandhi changed the face of an empire through his clear articulation of the importance of sovereignty for his people. Gandhi's beliefs, like Stalin's, were formed in his youth. They were reinforced in his early professional life.

Gandhi's belief in the right of his people to be treated without discrimination and his unwavering commitment to nonviolence produced results for India and the world that are still felt to this day. He sacrificed for his beliefs, ultimately paying with his life, but not before transforming the jewel of the British crown into the independent states of India and Pakistan. Consider this quote from Gandhi: "Nonviolence is the greatest force at the disposal of mankind. It is mightier than the mightiest weapon of destruction devised by the ingenuity of man."

Gandhi's belief in nonviolence as a transformative power was absolute! Even today notable leaders such as Nelson Mandela have followed in his steps to experience that power at work.

Stalin and Gandhi represent two vastly different approaches to leadership. Though most of us would consider Gandhi's approach good and Stalin's evil, my point is not in the morality or ethics of their leadership. My point is that the leadership each man displayed came from his character, and at the core of his character stood his Faith—the beliefs through which he saw the world, the beliefs that motivated his leadership.

So What?

It is one thing to look back on historical characters whose behavior is almost always enhanced by the passage of time. It is quite another to look clear-eyed at our contemporary leaders and, more importantly, at our own character and the leadership that arises from it.

At the end of each chapter, you will be encouraged to examine and reflect on a group of behaviors for each element of the character model. A serious leader will use these to ask questions about his character.

At the least, these behaviors create an assessment against which leaders and their teams can evaluate the leadership strength of each character element, with the idea that each of the behaviors can be enhanced or developed over time. At the most, the listed behaviors provide guideposts for encouraging, developing and maintaining the character of leadership.

The Leadership Behaviors of Faith

Many times our words and actions are not in alignment. The ability to **communicate through words a clear set of positive core beliefs** is a hallmark of great leadership. When this leadership behavior is combined with the next behavior, a leader demonstrates integrity. It is not our purpose to advocate for specific beliefs, but in our work we have found that the authenticity of a leader's alignment of words and actions is a powerful tool.

Talk is cheap! Leaders serious about developing their character and leadership will realize that it is easy to state beliefs, but a very different challenge entirely to **demonstrate those positive core beliefs in action.** This behavior contemplates that the leader has taken stock of his beliefs and articulated those beliefs in writing.

It is increasingly important in complex organizations for leaders to **provide clear meaning to the work of others.** Meaning motivates people. Meaning fosters trust when leaders deliberately show how the work of people links to and advances the vision of the organization.

When leaders are confident in their beliefs, they are not immediately thrown off guard by opposing views, and they **demonstrate openness to new ideas that may initially appear to contradict their beliefs.** Based on this openness they may even find reasons to refine their own views.

Chapter Three

Justice

*"Doing what is right, even
when it is difficult and costly."*

Justice is the seat of the leader's ethics. Ethics are the
behaviors that arise from a person's definition of right and
wrong; therefore, of all the aspects of a leader's character,
none is more obvious in its need and in its absence than
Justice. Justice is the filter through which leaders
demonstrate character when dealing with people.

We often focus on the behavior of leaders to determine
whether they are ethical or unethical. Of course, that
determination presupposes that the leader shares our view
of right and wrong. In fact, ethics by themselves are
qualitatively neutral, which reinforces why it is critical to
understand the leader's Faith.

Consider a person who believes stealing from a
stranger is acceptable. When that person does steal from a

stranger, they behave ethically, based on their definition of right and wrong. Conversely, a person who believes that stealing is wrong in all circumstances and consequently refrains from stealing is also acting ethically.

There are two reasons for using the term Justice rather than ethics to describe this leadership behavior. First, Justice stays true to the model put forth by great philosophers. Second and more importantly, Justice is more robust than ethics; it holds leaders to a higher standard regarding their actions. There is a proactive component to the word Justice that should challenge all leaders to think beyond ethical checklists.

In my office, I keep a copy of Webster's New International Dictionary, Second Edition, published in 1934—one of those huge dictionaries that used to dominate the tables of school libraries. I return to this dictionary often because its definitions hearken to a time when words seemed to have richer meaning. I looked to it for an understanding of the word "justice." I found that justice has two powerful but different meanings. First, justice is "the maintenance or administration of what is just (fair) by the impartial adjustment of conflicting claims."

In this usage, think of the legal system, established to redress wrongs. Every culture contains a system that helps people receive justice for the ills that have befallen them.

The second definition of justice, and the one we will use, is this: "the principle or ideal of just dealing or right action; conformity to this principle or ideal; conformity to truth, fact or reason."

This is the more challenging and less systematic view of justice. It is here we find the challenge for leaders to proactively demonstrate behaviors that are consistent with the beliefs articulated as part of Faith.

Doing Justice

Simply put, there two distinct differences in the above definitions: One means to "get justice" through some system of fairness, and the other means to "do Justice" in the constantly shifting circumstances in which leaders find themselves. Doing Justice means proactively doing what is right even when it is difficult and costly. Rarely is this behavior demonstrated more clearly than in the heroic story of Rosa Parks.

Rosa Parks Doing Justice

It was an ordinary workday in Montgomery, Ala., when a 42-year-old black woman paid her bus fare and sat down. As the bus filled with passengers, a white man insisted that she relinquish her seat. Rosa Parks refused and remained seated. That one decision set off a chain of events that eventually led to the collapse of institutional segregation on public transportation in the South.

On that December day in 1955, Rosa Parks did not board the bus to get arrested; she merely wanted to go home. When she refused to leave her seat, the bus driver had her arrested. The news reported she was physically tired, but she was no more tired than usual. She was, however, tired of the mistreatment and knew it was not right. Eventually she was tried and convicted of violating a city ordinance.

Like most segregation laws, those governing the bus system were complex and humiliating. Black passengers were required to pay their bus fare at the front of the bus, then get off and re-board through the back door. Occasionally the bus driver would drive off before the paid customer had a chance to get back on, leaving them behind. Once on the bus, if the white section was full and another white passenger entered the bus, black passengers were required to go back farther. If that was not bad enough, the laws also prohibited a black passenger from sitting across the aisle from a white passenger.

Rosa's arrest and conviction triggered a 381-day bus boycott in Montgomery as well as other cities. The little-known Dr. Martin Luther King, Jr. became the spokesman for the boycott and taught nonviolence to all who participated

Finally, in November 1956, the United States Supreme Court ruled that segregation on transportation was unconstitutional.

Although history gives credit to Rosa Parks for being "the Mother of the Civil Rights Movement," she always acknowledged that she did not do it alone. Her act of doing Justice was truly an inside-out proposition that was not only difficult and costly but eventually allowed for others to receive Justice as well.

No Small Feat

For leaders, doing Justice is no small feat and in fact may represent one of the most challenging elements of a leader's character. Stories abound of leaders of all ages and stations who have breached the trust of those they lead by acting in ways that are contrary to the beliefs of the organization and its people. The scandals caused by these leaders stretch from Wall Street to Main Street, from the statehouse to the pulpit.

The natural but inadequate reaction to these betrayals is to insist on new laws and regulations, all of which are well intentioned but will inevitably fall short of redressing the damage or correcting the cause of these failures. Incensed victims go looking for justice from the system established to control bad behavior. But what does getting justice really do in the long run? Almost nothing. Instead of accepting an endless flow of legislation and complicated regulations, we need to develop leaders who understand that one of their primary responsibilities is to do Justice so that no one needs to get justice.

The cost of the current approach is staggering. Consider the resulting legislation and prison terms handed down because of corporate excess. The backlash from Congress for the failures in public companies, beginning with Enron, resulted in the Sarbanes-Oxley legislation, which intended to create transparency and accountability. This body of legislation in essence made it illegal to lie, cheat, and steal—all things that were illegal before the Enron, Anderson, and Tyco scandals. The cost of complying with this legislation is staggering, and it will not elevate leadership above the mire of graft and corruption. The only thing that will improve things in the end is for leaders to learn and apply the simple phrase, "My role as a leader means I must do what is right for all involved, even when it is difficult and costly."

Does this approach seem too simple? Absolutely, but it is not because simplicity places greater demands on us than does complexity. The simplicity of the statement requires leaders to think, not just act. In her book, *Finding Our Way: Leadership for an Uncertain Time,* Margaret Wheatley shares the story of a junior high school that operates with three simple rules that apply to students, faculty, and staff. Those rules are:

1. Take care of yourself.
2. Take care of each other.
3. Take care of this place.

She goes on to share that one day a fire drill turned the entire school out into the rain, and once people were allowed to reenter the building, the principal noticed 800 pairs of shoes at the front entrance. No one needed to tell the students to remove their shoes when they were wet because the students were equipped to make those decisions based on the third rule of the school: Take care of this place.

What if we chose such a simple set of rules for leaders and said, "You can only make choices in which the rules are in harmony. If a choice fails to satisfy one of the rules, then you must find an alternative."

Let me share a personal experience of doing Justice, where we used one simple rule to navigate a complex set of problems. Banking is not a popular or beloved profession. Bankers are conservative, stuffy, and sometimes cold in their approach to business. It was in this atmosphere that I was schooled and in which I worked for seventeen years.

One of my roles during the mid-1980s was to act as the legal officer for the bank. This meant that I interacted with our attorneys in protecting the interests of the bank. It also meant that I was one of the key decision-makers in situations where the bank was sued. That time period saw a rise in legal conflicts with banks, based on the theory that banks could be held liable if they interfered too deeply with a borrower's business and consequently caused harm.

As borrowers won major awards in cases of "lender liability," it became more and more popular to sue banks, and I found myself, along with our attorneys, in the midst of several substantial lawsuits. Other banks in our marketplace had fallen to major awards from juries. So it was within this context that I was responsible for clearing up the various suits that had been filed against the bank.

Our first rule in meeting this challenge was to arrive at solutions without going to court. This rule was not wholly altruistic. We conceived it knowing that going to court to defend the bank had three potential costs: attorney fees, our time, and a tarnished public image. We knew that defending ourselves publicly would be expensive on all three fronts. Therefore, our approach was to resolve these disputes as business challenges rather than legal ones.

The other important factor that played into our strategy was that in some cases the borrowers were right about the bank's failures. Our hands were not always clean in these situations, and as a result, some of the grievances filed against us had merit. I do not believe that any of the bank's actions were intentionally reckless or motivated by malice, but nonetheless some of our actions had caused harm. Therefore, our approach, based on doing what was right for those who felt they had been wronged, was to enter into negotiations and find equitable settlements. Put simply, we attempted to do Justice rather than get justice.

The Story of Karl Plagge

The example of doing Justice at the bank is a pragmatic look at how leaders play this element out in daily activity. It pales in comparison to the Justice demonstrated by a little known Nazi by the name of Karl Plagge. Michael Good tells the story in his book, *The Search for Major Plagge*. Karl Plagge joined the Nazi Party in 1931 as Germany was attempting to recover economically and politically from the burden of war reparations after World War I. He saw in the Nazi party the pride of Germany being renewed.

Karl continued as a member even though disturbed by the rise of Adolf Hitler. Karl naively believed the party would eventually isolate the radical few whom Hitler represented and the merits of the Nazis would win out. Of course, his efforts and those of many others were not enough to outweigh the lunacy of Hitler and his cronies. Once again, Germany was plunged into war. Karl was drafted to serve as an army captain and eventually given command of the auto and truck repair facility, HKP 562, at Vilna, Poland.

It was at Vilna that Karl saw firsthand the genocide of the Jewish people by the Nazis. As commander of HKP 562, Karl had the power to exempt from extermination Jews deemed "essential" to the war effort. During his time as commander, he issued over one thousand such certificates, saving many lives.

In addition to issuing "essential" certificates, Karl ordered his men to treat all the workers humanely. He even allowed a substantial underground market among the workers so they could attempt to supplement their meager provisions. Karl undertook these actions unilaterally, without sharing his intentions, in order to save the lives of his workers. He did this at tremendous personal risk, since all camps that housed the "enemy" were under the direct command of the Nazi secret police, the SS.

As Germany's defeat in the war became evident and the Russian army advanced against them across Eastern

Europe, the Nazis' pattern was to exterminate their prisoners just before the Russians arrived at the camps. It was under this threat that Karl gathered all of his camp workers together in the presence of an SS officer one evening to issue a not-too-veiled warning. He said the Russians would soon be arriving in Vilna, and that the workers would be "escorted during this evacuation by the SS, which as you know, is an organization devoted to the protection of refugees. Thus, there's nothing to worry about."

The prisoners took this for the warning it was intended to be and as many as 250 of them escaped that very night. After the war, Karl stood trial as a war criminal and many of those who had survived because of him came forward and testified on his behalf. Although the court was prepared to acquit him, Karl insisted that he was not guiltless because he should have done more to help those in his charge. He lived out his life in obscurity and in 1959 died at the age of 59.

The Justice that Karl accomplished for those workers might never have come to light if not for the work of Michael Good. Michael's search for the man who saved his parents' lives while they were workers in HKP 562 led to Karl's inclusion in the Holocaust Museum of Israel as one of the "righteous among the nations" on April 10, 2005, an honor held by only a few just people.

We have offered three examples of the type of Justice that we challenge leaders to demonstrate. Perhaps your opportunity will be more heroic than the example from banking. Perhaps you will be challenged like Rosa Parks or Karl Plagge. Regardless of your situation, there are opportunities to demonstrate the Justice that is part of your character. Here are the behaviors related to the leader's sense of Justice.

The Leadership Behaviors of Justice

For those committed to developing this aspect of their character and leadership we offer the following behaviors:

Seizing opportunities to do what is right, even if not personally rewarding. The opportunity to do the right thing often occurs when we least expect it. Leaders must be diligent in observing those opportunities and seizing them. There is a selfless aspect to a leader's Justice as well. Leaders who are serious about doing Justice look for opportunities to do what is right for the organization and for others over and above their personal interests, demonstrating humility based on a sense of duty and responsibility, and doing so with a cheerful demeanor.

Leaders serious about Justice will **establish simple and clear guidelines for people to follow.** These guidelines provide the boundaries within which people can operate. Once these guidelines are established, leaders work diligently to **assure that team members can make just judgments for themselves within guidelines** without relying on the leader.

Just leaders accept **accountability for their own efforts and for the actions of others** without shrinking under the weight of that responsibility. Even though leaders are responsible for the actions of their teams, they must also be willing to **hold others accountable for their actions.**

The essence of being proactive is to **ensure that people receive fair treatment and equal opportunity** by constantly looking for potential inequities in treatment and opportunity and attempting to avert the negative consequences of inequities before they arise.

Practicing these behaviors will not guarantee that the leader will always be just. After all, we are human and thus given to certain imperfections and inconsistencies. But the challenge is worth undertaking to be a leader who does Justice.

Chapter Four

Temperance

"Temperance is actively demonstrating moderation and self-control in my life and my leadership."

We don't live in a moderate society! Considering the images and messages that are played continually for our ears and eyes—telling us to "Just do it," "Go for the gusto," and "Be all you can be"—it is amazing that we show any restraint whatsoever.

It was tempting to use another name for this particular element of character because, at least for students of 20th century American history, the word "temperance" is often associated with the "temperance movement," which saw the constitutional amendment banning the consumption of alcohol and the subsequent repeal of that amendment some 13 years later. In that vein, the word "temperance" is often associated with cold-hearted, self-righteous, and pious abstinence. The temperance movement became a failed social experiment in the legislative restraint of people's natural inclinations.

Why did it fail? From a public health viewpoint the abolition of alcohol or any mind-altering substance is a viable cause. There is ample proof that the overuse of alcohol and drugs can be detrimental. The human and financial cost to society would likely make it good public policy to ban all mind-altering substances. But movements like Prohibition assume that simply making something illegal will curb individual behavior. Alas, history proves that assumption false.

This is not to say that laws banning such substances might not have a dampening effect on some individual usage, but a law alone won't create Temperance. In fact, laws alone will only serve to drive a particular act underground. For Prohibition to have been successful, it would have needed to combine legislation with real desire on the part of the nation to abstain from using alcohol. There was no such campaign.

Let's contrast the temperance movement with a current equivalent: the environmental movement. The environmental movement is hardly new. We can look at history and see that people as far back as 1847 have been keenly aware of our need to protect the natural surroundings that we depend on for survival.

The movement has been bolstered by legislation that protects air, water, forests, and wildlife, and yet those laws alone were not effective for changing the views of Americans toward the environment. Coupled with the legislation was a drumbeat of environmental education that began in the public schools.

This generational approach to the ills of our consumptive behavior taught us why protecting the environment is important to the world, the nation, and to each of us individually. The barrage of information eventually seeped into the leadership of business, government, and nonprofit organizations, and years of legal and societal change have now created a country that is keenly interested in protecting the environment in ways that don't hinder our individual liberty but in fact enhance it.

Corporations are learning that it is pragmatic to embrace the "green" agenda, because it makes great sense for profit and shareholder wealth. It has taken several generations, but now we are collectively aware of and have a desire to do what is right for our environment. In other words, we are beginning to temper our behavior toward our environment.

According to Webster's dictionary, Temperance means "to moderate one's behavior or demonstrate self-control." Both of these meanings have important requirements for leaders, but before we discuss them, it is important to talk about what Temperance does not mean. Temperance is not being passive, passionless, or behaving like a milquetoast. It is the mixture of self-control and passion that has seen the rise of some of the most powerful leaders the world has ever known. History is dominated by men and women who have demonstrated Temperance combined with such passion for their causes that they literally saw the world transformed during their lives, making contributions that will better humanity for generations to come.

People like Mother Teresa and Martin Luther King, Jr. come to mind, along with one of the most fascinating leaders of any century, Mohandas K. Gandhi. What captivates us about Gandhi as a leader is that he held no elected or appointed leadership role during his time in India. He had been groomed as a social advocate during the oppression of Indians in South Africa, where he practiced law for 21 years.

Upon Gandhi's return to India in 1916, he turned his attention toward the injustice of British occupation of his native land and over the course of 32 years would wrest from the arms of the empire the jewel of its imperial crown. He did this, not by arming a militia and marching on British garrisons, but by joining Indians together in nonviolent marches and protests that proved so effective the British had no choice but to leave.

Gandhi's leadership arose from a clear set of core beliefs. The actions that stemmed from those beliefs were so powerful that he created a movement that overthrew the British Empire's rule of India. It is important to note that although Gandhi showed Temperance in the use of force against the British, he was not lukewarm toward his cause. Just the opposite: He was driven with a passion that consumed his life and that actually cost him his life at the hands of an assassin.

Gandhi suffered mightily at the hands of the British. They failed to see that he was a leader who would lay down his life for his cause. They imprisoned him to coerce his compliance to the British rule. This action made Gandhi a martyr in the eyes of his followers and fueled their collective passion for the cause. Despite all of

Britain's efforts, the rebellion would not be quashed. Gandhi, a shy and principled man, wrestled the jewel of the crown from the Empire through passionate, noncoercive means.

The key to Temperance is not restraining oneself against the furies that plague us on a daily basis. That sort of constant restraint ultimately fails because it focuses too narrowly on acting and not deeply enough on changing core behaviors. Most of us can demonstrate that type of restraint for a short period, but ultimately what is on the inside spills out and our true nature becomes all too apparent. Loss of self-control often happens in highly charged situations and leads to deflated leadership and embarrassment.

Humility: The Root of Temperance

The key to genuine Temperance is personal humility. Humility is an underrated leadership attribute and one that desperately needs cultivating among many of the egocentric leaders often considered "impressive."

The great leaders whom Jim Collins describes in his book *Good to Great* were a mysterious mixture of personal humility and professional will. This combination may seem like a contradiction at first glance, but it makes great sense upon reflection. Collins calls this leadership "level-five leadership."

After much research, Collins and his team determined that the leaders of "good to great" companies were CEOs who could cultivate organizations that out-perform competitors in any context. This takes a relentless pursuit of the organization's objectives. It also requires recognition that people follow leaders who take their roles seriously without taking themselves seriously.

Level-five leaders understand the critical role they play in marshalling the team and the resources for success. They also have enough self-awareness to realize that they don't have a corner on good ideas or on the skills necessary to achieve the results.

I spent most of my banking career working for a level-five leader. The chairman of the bank was a gentleman who took his role very seriously. He brought together a series of successful acquisitions in a way that preserved the best talent from each organization. He made some very courageous decisions about expansion but only after careful consideration and debate among the senior leadership.

Those of us who worked for him never forgot he was the chairman of the board. We never saw him take credit for the accomplishments of the bank without publicly thanking the team (from top to bottom) that had made success possible. Many times he would admit that if he had any talent at all, it was his ability to attract and retain the right people for the jobs the bank needed done. Since I was one of those people, I took this as both a compliment and as permission to do my job in ways that fostered our collective success. The behaviors I saw from this man could best be categorized as Temperance, self-control, and moderation. The root of his Temperance was personal humility.

Discipline is another dimension of Temperance. While humility is mostly instinctive, discipline is the focusing of the mind to deliberately avoid thoughts, language, and actions that could undermine Temperance. Like constant restraint, discipline alone is not sufficient to guide leadership behavior. Eventually discipline will let a leader down if he or she relies only on that aspect of Temperance.

Examples of the failure of Temperance that stems from discipline without humility are most often found in those politicians, executives, and clergy who espouse a certain restrained approach to life, politics, or business. They are often very vocal in their disdain for people who don't share their views. Many times these leaders' careers end in shame and ruin as the public discovers they were actually engaging in the very practices they were vehemently condemning in others.

There are undoubtedly developmental and psychological reasons for this type of duplicitous behavior but from a character and leadership perspective, it is easy to observe that the Temperance they displayed relied on discipline and control without the necessary mix of humility and discipline. Humility by itself has a tempering effect on character and the leadership to which it gives rise.

The Leadership Behaviors of Temperance

The Temperance necessary for leadership is a mix of humility and discipline. Here are the behaviors to guide Temperance.

A temperate leader **listens attentively to others without reacting with emotional outbursts.** True leaders know that the flow of information is critical to the organization's success and so they must remain receptive to all conversations, especially ones that convey disturbing information. Demonstrating this behavior well will build trust with followers and allow the leader to continually **invite contact by being open and approachable.**

Temperate leaders **remain calm and deal fairly with all people in high-pressure situations.** This behavior is particularly telling. It is usually under pressure that we discover what is truly inside us.

It is easy for leaders to take credit for success because they are often the focus of public celebrations. Although there is nothing wrong with celebrating a leader's success, a truly temperate leader will **remain focused on results without seeking personal credit for success and make sure that success is shared with the team.**

Temperance of character that allows a leader to moderate his or her behavior and demonstrate self-control is a powerful and compelling leadership tool.

Chapter Five

Hope

*"Hope is sincerely and convincingly
articulating a bright future,
especially when the immediate
circumstances are bleak."*

Hope is one of the most powerful drivers of the human spirit and one of the essential ingredients of human existence. Without Hope, people die.

Viktor Frankl was a young Viennese neurologist and psychiatrist when the Nazis confined him, his wife, and other members of his family to the concentration camps. Frankl's wife and many other family members died in those camps. His own death was narrowly thwarted when he took advantage of a guard's lack of attention: He moved from the line he was in, which was headed to the gas chamber, to the line that was headed for the barracks.

During the three years he spent in four camps, Frankl observed how some prisoners survived. He wrote that the key ingredient in his own survival, aside from luck, was his willingness to search for and find meaning. He learned that the most powerful motivator a person can have is to find meaning in any circumstance, no matter how egregious. Meaning creates hope, and hope leads people to endure and achieve.

Most leaders deal with matters more mundane and routine than life and death, but it is no stretch to say that without the Hope cultivated by a leader's essential spirit, the "life" of the organization will slowly and inexorably be lost. Napoleon said, "A leader is a dealer in hope." This is certainly the contention here. Leaders must cultivate Hope in themselves in order to be able to cultivate it in their teams and organizations.

Hope is a fixed expectation of a future that is brighter than the present. From a leadership standpoint, it is the lifeblood of organizations. Cultivating Hope is really a matter of weaving pragmatism and vision. Hope is the state of mind that recognizes possibilities and opportunities for the future while staying grounded in the realities and circumstances of the present.

Pragmatism: Hope's Footing

It seems right at this point to share a story of optimism—the naïve, unbridled, rosy-colored variety—as a way of illustrating what happens when pragmatism is missing from Hope. We worked with a small enterprise that was led by its entrepreneurial founder. The owner had been reasonably successful in managing the company as it grew to nearly one hundred employees. As the company grew beyond that point, it was clear there were leadership challenges that were beyond the owner's abilities.

When the company suffered an economic reversal due to a change in strategy by its largest customer, the owner decided that the best way to use the company's finite resources was to look for clients who would single-handedly repair the company's financial ills. This meant the sales team was constantly trying to land large accounts in markets in which they had little experience. Soon a cloud of defeat settled over the employees. Suggestions that the company make small sales in the local market using products it already had perfected were rejected out of hand as not being lofty enough to both heal the company and (although this was never said) satisfy the ego requirements stemming from the owner's former brush with success.

The result was that the company continued to struggle because it was ruled by naïve optimism rather than Hope. Pragmatism was missing, and so every time the attempt to land the big client failed, the employees suffered defeat. This drained rather than instilled energy and enthusiasm. In addition, the team lost respect for the owner because he appeared detached from the brutal reality of his situation.

Vision: Hope's Wings

To build and foster Hope in the organization a leader must ensure there is a clear, shared vision of the future. This requires making sure that the vision is realistic while stretching the people in the organization to achieve something together that they could not achieve separately. A vision should capture the underlying meaning of the organization in a way that expands the imagination of the people without discouraging them. It takes practice to achieve this balance.

I once heard a speaker say, "The difference between a hallucination and a vision is the number of people who see it." A vision must by definition be something that everyone can see, understand, and, most importantly, commit to.

In 1962 President John F. Kennedy set a vision for the nation when he asked Congress for the funding to send a man to the moon before the end of the decade. He summarized this vision in a speech at Rice University:

▌▌ *But if I were to say, my fellow citizens, that we shall send to the moon 240,000 miles away from the control station in Houston a giant rocket more than 300 feet tall—the length of this football field—made of new metal alloys some of which have not yet been invented, capable of standing heat and stresses several times more than have ever been experienced, fitted together with a precision better than the finest watch, carrying all the equipment needed for propulsion, guidance, control, communications, food, and survival, on an untried mission, to an unknown celestial body and then return it safely to earth re-entering the atmosphere at speeds of over 25,000 miles per hour, causing heat about half that of the temperature of the sun—almost as hot as it is here today—and do all this and do it right and do it first before this decade is out—then we must be bold.* ▌▌

Was Kennedy's space challenge hallucination or vision? Looking over the last 47 years, it is clear that this vision was an inspired way to galvanize a nation mired in the Cold War to reach for something that would transcend the current tension between the West and the Soviet Bloc.

Winston Churchill used the same power of vision when he mobilized Britain and the Western world against the Axis nations. He was on the front lines of the conflict long before the American public understood the ramifications of Hitler's march across Europe. In a frightening and hopeful speech before the House of Commons on June 18, 1940, Churchill solemnly described the end of the Battle of France while demonstrating the confidence and vision necessary to lead his nation into the coming Battle of Britain:

What General Weygand called the Battle of France is over. I expect that the Battle of Britain is about to begin. Upon this battle depends the survival of Christian civilization. Upon it depends our own British life, and the long continuity of our institutions and our Empire. The whole fury and might of the enemy must very soon be turned on us. Hitler knows that he will have to break us in this Island or lose the war. If we can stand up to him, all Europe may be free and the life of the world may move forward into broad, sunlit uplands. But if we fail, then the whole world, including the United States, including all that we have known and cared for, will sink into the abyss of a new Dark Age made more sinister, and perhaps more protracted, by the lights of perverted science. Let us therefore brace ourselves to our duties, and so bear ourselves that, if the British Empire and its Commonwealth last for a thousand years, men will still say, "This was their finest hour."

What was the combination of attributes that allowed Kennedy and Churchill to articulate Hope for their respective peoples? To begin with, they were men driven by lofty ideals and pragmatic truths. However, they were not bound by one or the other of those twin attributes. Leaders often have a tendency toward either vision or pragmatism but not both. It would be useless to argue which is most important because they are both critical. The challenge for the leader is to be able to draw on both of these, although they seem mutually exclusive. To do so requires that a leader grapple and become comfortable with the burden of pragmatism and the ambiguity of vision. In order to make that grappling easier we have delineated the behaviors that leaders must develop to convey Hope to their people.

The Leadership Behaviors of Hope

A hopeful leader recognizes that cultivating Hope is a long-term proposition that may not deliver short-term results. A leader must deal with that tension on a daily basis by **leading with a sense of purpose that transcends the immediate.**

Hopeful leaders realize that the launch pad for the organization's vision is the reality of its current situation. So, **ask questions that challenge current thinking; explore and question accepted practices, patterns and assumptions; and stimulate creativity.**

Many leaders are concerned that they may not personally possess a vision for the organization. Leaders must **assure that the organization has a clear and compelling vision of the future** but they do not have to develop it themselves. Developing vision is a team event.

Even though leaders do not need to personally develop the vision for the organization, they are primarily responsible for **communicating the vision in a way that promotes wide ownership.**

Leaders need to share the story of how people's work ties to the vision to **ensure that everyone's actions are consistent with the vision and support its achievement.**

Chapter Six

Wisdom

"Wisdom is applying my accumulated knowledge and experience effectively to situations."

It would be a mistake to address the subject of Wisdom without discussing King Solomon. Most are familiar with the story of the two women who went before the king, each claiming a particular infant as their own. Long before DNA could have solved the problem for him, Solomon demonstrated his incomparable Wisdom by offering to have the child cut in half, providing equal portions of the child to each woman. This offer elicited a quick response from the child's real mother, who gladly gave up her claim to save the child's life.

Solomon's famous Wisdom is said to have come to him following a conversation with God in which God offered him anything he desired. The young king had the presence of mind to ask for Wisdom above all else. (Obviously, he already possessed some Wisdom because this choice alone was wise.)

What makes Wisdom so valuable? Wisdom allows you to apply your experience, and the collective experience of others, to the most challenging leadership situations. Solomon knew this and pursued the acquisition of Wisdom as part of his character. We should do the same.

Because Wisdom is such an important facet of a leader's character, we will break the behavior into three components for study, understanding, and development. The three components are self-awareness, knowledge, and action.

Self-Awareness

To cultivate the self-awareness that builds Wisdom, you need to spend time understanding your own nature, background, and worldview. Each of these has played an important role in developing your leadership philosophy and leadership style. Most people don't really understand this. Becoming aware of how you gather, process, and act on information is critical for gaining Wisdom.

It is not enough to recognize the obvious, that each of us has strengths and weaknesses. From a leadership standpoint, what counts is knowing what those strengths and weaknesses are, emphasizing the strengths, and compensating for the weaknesses. For many years leadership development advocated teaching leaders to overcome their weaknesses. Normal improvement not withstanding, to the extent these "weaknesses" are part of our nature there is very little anyone can or should do to overcome them. Shortcomings that can be attributed to the leader's background or world view can be changed if in fact they are inhibiting the growth of leadership.

To make the point about self-awareness even more acutely, let's explore a leadership condition that is the antithesis of self-awareness, narcissism. Fortunately, we don't often encounter this condition in its full bloom in our consulting engagements. But when we do, we can see that the effects of narcissism are tragically debilitating to the team and destructive to the organization.

Narcissism is an over-inflated sense of self with a constant need to be esteemed, where the person believes he or she is superior to others and has little regard for their feelings. A narcissistic leader generally communicates a lack of respect for the team and exhibits disingenuous behavior that undermines the expertise of the team's best people, which ultimately leads to organizational mediocrity or destruction. This leader surrounds himself with only those willing to submit to his inflated view of his own skills and abilities.

We have seen this leadership style only twice in ten years. Both times, the organizations had a clear vision, a compelling plan, and a strong team. Both were led by charming narcissists who had to be involved in every decision and informed of every issue, and who would eventually undermine the responsibility of their most capable team members. This form of leadership is a perverted way of demonstrating self-importance and the illusion of superiority. What makes the charming narcissist so dangerous is not just his lack of self-awareness but the illusion he projects of actually being self-aware. He invites debate and discussion while all the time knowing deep down that he will pursue his own path anyway.

These leaders would benefit from a quick reading of *The Emperor's New Clothes* by Hans Christian Andersen. Remember the tale? A narcissistic king is convinced his new clothes are the most wonderful in all the land because a conniving tailor has supposedly sewn the clothes from invisible thread. But in fact there are no clothes at all, and the king wanders the streets completely naked. It takes a small child to speak the truth to the king, who is at first aghast and then embarrassed by his gaffe.

No matter the type of organization you lead, you will find lasting results and satisfaction only if you embrace the challenge of becoming intimately and realistically self-aware enough to develop a humble and driven approach to your character and thus your leadership. If you will admit your nakedness (which, by the way, everyone around you already sees) before your people, they will embrace your honesty. For the record: As leaders, we are all naked.

Knowledge

The second component of Wisdom is the willingness and ability of a leader to accumulate the knowledge that is critical to tackling the organization's most challenging situations. Leaders must be avid students of their environment, rather than mere commentators on the events in their organization; they must be curious observers of what works and what does not work. Accumulation of knowledge is a critical element in the development of Wisdom and the character of leadership. This also means looking outside the organization and the leader's immediate experiences. The willingness to remain teachable allows for unrestrained leadership growth and team development. A teachable spirit lets the leader avoid becoming a limiting force in the organization. This happens when a leader essentially caps the team's and the organization's growth by stagnating in his leadership.

Action

Leaders must be action-oriented to navigate the challenges that confront them and take advantage of the opportunities that emerge daily. From a Wisdom perspective, merely having knowledge is not enough. You must also be willing to take risks, act independently, and make use of plans to align resources and activities.

Lincoln's Wisdom

Perhaps no American president has been scrutinized more than Abraham Lincoln. His presidency during one of our nation's most critical periods brought him both contempt and praise from his contemporaries.

Now nearly 150 years beyond his death, we still attempt to understand what made this man such a great leader. From our perspective, there is one quality in Lincoln's leadership that stands above the rest: Wisdom.

Paramount among the numerous examples of Lincoln's wisdom was his appointment of adversaries and detractors to his cabinet. As he began to build his administration, Lincoln chose four men to play critical roles. These four represented the best minds the country had to offer, but they also were outspoken competitors of the new president. It took persuasion, but eventually Lincoln was able to get these men to accept his offers.

From a character perspective, it was Lincoln's Wisdom that compelled him to look to his political opponents to find the best leaders for the fledgling and shaky republic. Lincoln knew the needs of the country and his own strengths and weaknesses, and he knew the capabilities of these men, his political adversaries. Self-awareness coupled with accumulated and practical knowledge put into action are the qualities that made Lincoln the epitome of Wisdom.

The Leadership Behaviors of Wisdom

All of the elements of a leader's character are important and interwoven, but Wisdom stands as one of the most critical. Based on the three components of Wisdom, set against the background of Lincoln's challenging example, here is the list of behaviors for you to evaluate and apply to yourself.

A wise leader seeks to **understand his own strengths and exploits them for the good of the organization.** The result of seeking information and earnestly developing one's leadership is a deep understanding of one's own style and the impact (positive and negative) that one's style has on others.

Investing time and energy in self-development and growth is important from two standpoints. First, it shows a willingness to be in a continual growth mode as a leader. Second, it signals to the rest of the organization that such development is important and that no one is above the need for development.

Often the most valuable way to **expand one's knowledge is to explore information and experiences in other, often unrelated, fields.** This may seem counterintuitive, but many problems can be solved by looking at how others have met similar challenges. This can be especially true if you are part of an industry that is slow to adopt new trends. Look to the early adopters for their experiences.

Leading by walking around has long been a practice of successful leaders. The proactive approach of **seeking information from others** inside the organization by staying connected to them and visiting them in their workspaces is invaluable.

Looking before you leap is as great a lesson for leaders as it is for children. Too much leadership time is spent in action that has no clear purpose, so a wise leader **ensures that action plans are prepared and used.**

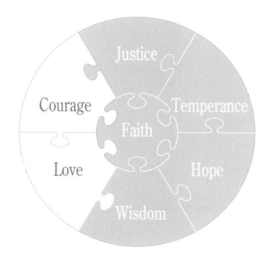

Chapter Seven

Love

"For the leader, love is demonstrating
a genuine concern, care, and compassion
for the people you lead and interact with."

The word "love" may be one of the most loaded words in the English language! I even considered finding a different term to describe this element of the character model just to avoid the distraction that could be caused by the misunderstanding of how Love displays itself in a leader's character. Upon further deliberation I thought that the strength of the word itself would help communicate just how important it is for a leader to cultivate this essential element.

Years ago we had the opportunity to work with a client who used our leadership development services to improve the capabilities of his new leaders and to help other leaders get their teams back on track. Such was the case when we received a call to coach Alex.

Alex, it turns out, had managed to alienate most of his

team members fairly quickly after taking over. The team considered Alex to be arrogant, aloof, and hard to communicate with.

The call came into our office to see if we could "fix Alex." Like good coaches we explained that the changes that would need to be made would have to be owned by Alex if they were going to be positive and lasting. We agreed to meet with him. Here's what happened:

Alex was introduced to his coach and entered the conference room. He began reciting a long list of his abilities and successes. He said he had been a major player in many multinational organizations and had almost single-handedly led each of them to success. He said that after he left each of those companies they fell on hard times—all because they no longer had the advantage of his stellar abilities. This monologue went on for two hours while the coach listened patiently.

Finally, Alex finished. He turned to the coach and said, "Well, I guess I need you to be my coach!" The coach replied, "Before I came into this room, I had a chance to gather some information about the feelings your team has toward your leadership. Your team believes that you believe 'it's all about you.' Now after two hours of listening to you,

I have to agree, so I am not going to be your coach, Alex."
Alex was a bit puzzled by this response but stayed quiet
while the coach finished. "Alex, you don't need a leadership
coach. You don't have a leadership problem; you have a
character problem. You see, Alex, you don't Love your
people. Consequently, until you do genuinely care about their
interests above your own you will not be able to lead them."

Alex may have been capable of learning the behaviors he
needed, and he might even have been able to act them out
for some period. But until he has a change of heart there will
be no growth in his leadership ability. Alex is not willing to
accept that he needs to Love his people in order to lead them.

You Must Love Your People in Order to Lead Them

What do we mean by this challenging statement? Our
definition of Love as a component of a leader's character is
"having a deep-seated care, compassion, and concern for
your people." Don't confuse this with "romance" or any
other behavior that advances beyond the acceptable in a
work environment. Love as a characteristic of leadership
challenges us to see our team members as people, first and
foremost.

The Character of Leadership

There is an interesting phrase often used by businesses that says, "Our people are our greatest asset." Although well meaning, the idea that people are "an asset" conveys a sense of ownership, objectification, and control that is neither desirable nor achievable when dealing with people.

The type of Love we are advocating is characterized by an interdependent relationship, one in which leader and follower share mutual respect and genuine human concern for one another. And when the challenges of life and work invade the team, the successful leader sees her team members first as people, with complex and interesting lives. Only secondarily does she see them as units of production. The result? Everyone is more productive.

Organizational systems expert Margaret Wheatley challenges us to separate our mechanistic views of organizations from the systems that are brought to life by people. Her contention (and she is right) that organizations are living systems, not mechanical ones, should resonate with all leaders as a call to see not only the complexities and challenges of the people side of the organization, but the amazing capacity that people have to shape something in which they believe.

When we talk of loving people from a leadership perspective, we mean Love on two levels. On a personal level, a leader must show the respect, compassion, care, and concern discussed above. On a corporate level, the leader must Love people in a more general sense. This more general Love comprises an intense respect for and fascination with the challenges and complexities that people bring to organizations. The successful leader will take on the challenge of understanding and releasing the abilities of people to find and maintain meaning in their work. In the final analysis, this will be both satisfying to employees and very profitable for the organization.

Like each of the other elements of leadership character, Love is made up of components worthy of individual study. The components of Love are selfless respect and shared trust.

Selfless Respect

Taking up the leadership mantle requires self-confidence. At the same time the best and most caring leaders demonstrate a selflessness that puts the needs of the team above their own needs for gratification.

I experienced this type of selfless behavior from the chairman of the holding company that owned the bank where I worked for eleven years. Victor Riley was known as a hard-driving man with a strong focus on bottom-line performance. He was also known for his ability to connect with the people in the bank, regardless of their positions.

I love being a leader, and as a banker my goal was to become CEO. I reached that goal in April of 1996 when my boss (the current CEO) was promoted to a role in a newly created division.

But my time at the top was short-lived. Within a few months the company reorganized and that new division was abolished. My former CEO returned to his old job, and I was demoted to the role of executive vice president.

I took the news in stride, but I was disappointed—my dream had been snatched away. It was not only a professional reversal but a personal crisis as well. As is true for so many of us, my identity was caught up in my work.

In the midst of my crisis of position and identity, Victor Riley, the bank's chairman of the board visited my community to speak at the local university. He asked that I pick him up at the airport, and it was during that ride that I experienced his selfless behavior. Victor asked me three questions. Although the questions were not unusual, the order in which they were asked made a permanent impression.

The questions were: ———————————————————

- How is your wife?
- How are your boys?
- How is your bank?

———————————————————————————————

As chairman, Victor had every right to lead with the question about the bank, but instead he asked about my family first. I really don't know if he remembered who my wife was or that I had two sons. For all I know, he had that information on a 3x5 card. I don't care how he remembered; I was just impressed that he demonstrated concern for me as a person. It was the kind of concern I needed from a leader with his position and power.

That selflessness illustrated his genuine care and concern for me and was the type of Love we are advocating that leaders demonstrate to their people.

Shared Trust

The second aspect of loving the people you lead is shared trust. The leader must take up the challenge of developing and maintaining trust. But trust must be mutual, demonstrated by both leader and follower.

Trust is the foundational component for all human relationships. Without trust, relationships are strained and dysfunctional. With trust, relationships are vibrant and powerful. Writing about trust is a challenge because it is difficult to see trust in the affirmative. In other words, it is easier to see trust when it is broken rather than when it is whole.

When asked to coach individuals and teams, we often find that if the leader or team is in trouble it is because trust has been broken—but the real problem is that the team did not define trust in the first place. In order to rebuild trust we spend time understanding the specifics of the situation, and then we have the team agree on what trust would look like if it were strong. From there we share four steps in building trust: *ask, negotiate, commit, and act.*

To build shared trust a leader must depend on the performance of others. That means that leaders must continually *ask* their followers to perform certain duties or take on projects. Therefore, the first step in building shared trust is to *ask* for something to be done.

The next step is to *negotiate* the task boundaries, quality, and timing. Even though leaders can "order" performance, building shared trust means asking followers for action and then actively negotiating the performance of that action. This means that followers are allowed to say "no" to certain tasks not because they simply refuse but because they want to make sure that they understand the request and can negotiate the outcome, timing and quality of the action. This is the step in which assumptions are eliminated and expectations are mutually established.

Step three is to *commit.* This allows each party to know that the other has made a clear decision to engage in the agreement.

Finally, *act.* This means completing the agreement to the specifications agreed to, in the time allotted, with the quality that was promised. The leader who wants to engender shared trust will first use these four steps in interactions with the team and will make sure that the team uses these steps as well.

Shared trust means the leader's cultivation of interdependence among team members. As a leader, you can foster the development of shared trust by asking for, negotiating, committing to, and performing acts with your team. The result will be a more efficient and productive environment that produces the best your team has to offer.

The Leadership Behaviors of Love

Demonstrating selfless respect and building shared trust with your team members is the essence of loving them. Love is the only reason that a leader would willingly commit to two such challenging and significant character elements. To be sure, a leader could achieve results without mastering either of these competencies, but without Love in your leadership, you are missing the opportunity for your organization to achieve its best performance.

Here are the behaviors that will demonstrate your Love for the people you lead:

When listening, **give full attention and show genuine interest.** This is one of the most obvious ways to demonstrate selfless respect. Listening is one of the most underrated and powerful leadership competencies.

Contrary to popular belief, leaders don't have all the answers. Those who **willingly accept questions and input from team members** are demonstrating selfless respect toward those they lead.

When children hurt each other physically or emotionally, they are taught to apologize. Leaders too should **offer genuine apologies when they say or do something inappropriate.**

Realizing that team members are people before they are employees, leaders **demonstrate a genuine concern for the lives of the people they lead.** Building shared trust requires the leader to **discuss and then openly negotiate with others their expectations of the leader's performance.** Following those negotiations, leaders **make specific commitments based on negotiated terms.** Leaders then **perform those commitments in a timely manner.**

Chapter Eight

Courage

*"Courage is not the
absence of fear."*

The role of fear as a limiting force in our lives is an immense subject but not the focus of this chapter. The focus here is Courage. As a leader, you must learn to cultivate this characteristic so that when fear strikes, Courage is ready to serve you.

As I have spoken on Courage over the years, I have come to understand that this is one of the most challenging of the character components for me. I have concluded that my struggle to exercise Courage is rooted in prosperity.

I have lived a privileged life without a lot of hardship. Compared to the people I worked with in Manila, I have never seen a very difficult day. My privilege has not been defined by enormous wealth but rather by the lack of real adversity. Consequently, when challenges have arisen for me as a leader, I have often wanted to run or at least change direction so that the obstacle could be avoided rather than confronted.

There is value in seeing the path around an obstacle, and in general, when leadership obstacles occur, it is valid to look for the alternatives. My shortcoming, however, is that I sometimes take the alternative route when the direct one—requiring firmness and boldness—would have been better. I deliberately circumvent obstacles to keep my life easy.

I know I am not alone in this. In order for me to overcome this leadership weakness, I must acknowledge it. Then I must take the challenging path even when escape routes present themselves. I find it particularly difficult to demonstrate the Courage of confrontation. I like being liked, and so there have been times when as a leader I have failed to take direct, decisive action.

My struggle with Courage manifested itself early in the operation of our consulting group. We had one major client that represented sixty percent of the revenue for our fledgling company. For five years, I worked closely with the owner/CEO, his family, and most of the company's leadership team. During that time, I got way too close to the action. I lost my objectivity and began to behave more as an employee of the company than a trusted advisor. When a consultant loses objectivity, a significant component of the value we provide disappears. I did not confront this issue even though in the back of my mind I knew it was time for me to leave.

I stayed on for a few extra months; I was afraid that I could not sustain the economic realities of losing my largest client. Finally in early spring, I mustered what Courage I had and fired myself as their consultant.

Over the past years I have reflected many times on why I waited so long. The answer is very simple: I lacked the Courage to lead forward, to face an obstacle with firmness, valor, and boldness.

Look to Others for Inspiration

One way to bolster Courage is to read stories of others who have faced and overcome obstacles with firmness, valor, and boldness. Stories of Courage large and small abound, but there is one that has captivated my imagination for a number of years. It is the story of Sir Ernest Shackleton's Imperial Trans-Antarctic Expedition.

Shackleton's story is one of failure, danger, despair, triumph, survival, and, especially, Courage—not just Shackleton's Courage but also the Courage of the men who followed him.

Shackleton was the most colorful of a trio of explorers (the other two were Robert Falcon Scott and Roald Amundsen) who made up the Golden Age of Polar Exploration.

Shackleton's first attempt to reach the South Pole was in 1901 when he and Scott led an expedition that came within 745 miles of its goal before being turned back by cold and starvation. Shackleton led his own quest for the pole in 1908, coming within 100 miles before being turned back again.

In 1910, Scott and Amundsen raced to the pole, each wanting to capture the honor for their respective countries. Amundsen reached it first and returned with his team intact to Norway. Scott also reached the pole but he and his men perished on the return trip.

Shackleton was left without a prize of his own to claim. Thus, he conceived the Imperial Trans-Antarctic Expedition, with the goal of being the first person to cross the Antarctic continent.

The ship Endurance and its 27-member crew left England on August 8, 1914, making its way to the island of South Georgia, a whaling outpost in the South Atlantic Ocean, and from there launching toward Antarctica. In the face of warnings about the risks of the year's unprecedented ice pack in the Weddell Sea (the expedition's launch point), Shackleton and crew pushed into the Weddell, only to find themselves soon frozen into the unyielding pack of ice.

The Endurance fought bravely against the superior power of the ice, but on October 15, 1915, Shackleton ordered the ship abandoned. His men, with their dogs, three lifeboats, and all the provision they could muster, found themselves stranded. The crew spent 497 days on the ice before they were able to find open water to launch the lifeboats in search of solid ground.

They finally found it in the form of Elephant Island. While the crew was elated to find safety, the unfortunate reality was that Elephant Island lay outside any shipping lanes. The only chance for survival would be to send out a few men in one of the lifeboats in search of South Georgia.

Shackleton launched the chancy attempt in the largest boat, 22.5 feet long. He took with him a handful of men and the navigator, who only got two sightings of the sun during the ten-day period that the boat was afloat. They found the island of South Georgia, but they landed on the opposite shore from the populated whaling station. Adding to the challenge, they broke the boat's tiller upon landing. This meant that they had to ascend the island's 10,000-foot peak to reach the whaling station on the other side. They did so, and with the help of the Argentine government mounted a rescue effort to return to Elephant Island.

As Shackleton and his fellow survivors approached Elephant Island, they scanned the beach for survivors. Shackleton, to his great joy, found all his men still alive.

Ernest Shackleton never led a successful expedition. All of his expeditions failed to meet the desired objectives, and yet those very failures illustrate for all of us the Courage that leaders must display to handle the continual challenges and obstacles in today's organizations.

Courage in Modern-Day Leadership

I witnessed courageous leadership early in my banking career when a client who had been very successful failed.

Bill was a truck dealer—in fact, one of the largest and

most successful truck dealers in the nation. The company enjoyed millions of dollars in revenue, generous compensation, and many accolades from manufacturers. However, despite early success not all was well inside the company. In spite of the desperate efforts of its young owners, the company collapsed, and the once-rising star leading the company found himself in the throes of bankruptcy.

During this same time I was in the midst of trying to establish myself as a banker and attract business to the bank. To my mix of horror and pleasure, my supervisor introduced me to Bill and suggested that I make him some loans so he could re-establish himself in business. Since bankers are taught to evaluate and mitigate risk, being introduced to a bankrupt borrower is horrifying. On the other hand I had loan goals to meet, and so I was pleased to talk to Bill and understand his needs. But I was hesitant, not having been involved in the failure and not knowing whether I could trust him. Nonetheless, loans were made and repaid, and that was the beginning of a strong business relationship and deep friendship. Some twenty years beyond his financial demise and resurrection, he and his wife have quietly amassed a substantial business. Moreover, this former truck dealer is now on the board of directors for a new bank recently founded by a group of investors.

Tests of a leader's Courage may happen on the battlefield or as part of an expedition where lives hang in the balance. Courage may also mean, as in Bill's case, perseverance in the face of insurmountable financial obstacles. The leaders we encounter in our work aren't facing life-threatening situations. But they still need Courage—the same Courage demonstrated by Ernest Shackleton and by Bill—to meet the challenges and take advantage of the opportunities that arise in their organizations.

The Leadership Behaviors of Courage

Translating Courage into character and leadership means understanding the specific behaviors that our examples in this chapter exhibited.

Courageous leaders **tackle conflict by making it clear to both parties why it's necessary to resolve it.** Bold leaders **make sure the most important and difficult issues are put on the table to be resolved.** Getting to the root of situations is a goal of bold leaders, and so they **encourage people to speak up and communicate directly when conflicts arise.**

When leaders have Courage, they **seize opportunities to avert risk or achieve success.**

Every leader encounters difficulty. It is simply part of the job description. Leaders with Courage **approach obstacles and challenges with determination to succeed.**

In order to stay fixed on goals, leaders must be able to **find a clear and direct path in ambiguous situations.**

Chapter Nine

Developing a
Leadership Legacy

*" A leader has a unique and
compelling reason to craft a legacy."*

Now that we have discussed each of the character
elements and their relationship to leadership, we must put
the model into action. Many labor under the assumption
that leaders are born with the skills necessary to lead.
Indeed some leaders are "born," but most of us have to
learn to lead effectively. The great news is that leadership
can indeed be learned.

It's important to understand that there are two separate
parts to leadership: style and competency. To be a
competent leader you must demonstrate specific,
identifiable behaviors. We view each of the character
elements as competencies that leaders must develop.
At the end of each chapter we shared the observable and
measurable behaviors related to each character element.

The other part of leadership is style. Style is the way in which the behaviors are demonstrated. A person's leadership style is a function of temperament and experience.

Leadership Style

Temperament is a well-understood component of psychology. The work of Carl Jung was popularized by the efforts of Isabel Myers and gave rise to innumerable assessments and descriptions of the four primary temperament types. Each temperament type gives rise to a different leadership style. In our work we use the popular DISCstyles™ assessment, which provides the basic building blocks of leadership style.

It is often the leader's style that people react to, but leadership is the mix of style and behaviors. An important distinction between these two terms is that behaviors are neutral to temperament and as such are simpler to learn. They are neutral to the style that is applied by the leader. Style, on the other hand, is "hard-wired," and although it can be modified by learning, experience, and maturity, it is a fixed component of leadership.

Behaviors of a Competent Leader

It is critical to understand this separation of style and behavior and to make sure that leadership behaviors—or the lack thereof—are not overruled by temperament. Leadership behaviors are learned and as such can be changed and molded over time based on the desire of the leader and the needs of the leadership role.

Becoming a leader is like getting a role in a movie. The role requires that an actor appear in certain ways in certain circumstances and remain in character for the duration of the filming. This is just like the behavioral part of leadership. On the other hand, even though the actor is behaving one way in front of the camera, this role has not changed his underlying temperament.

Now don't take this metaphor too far. I am not suggesting that leading is acting, not letting people know your real self. There are times in which a leader must fill a role even though it may not be her personal style or flow naturally from her innate temperament. That is when the successful leader calls upon the behaviors that we have outlined for each of the elements of character. These foundational behaviors will give rise to the acts of leadership, even when it does not come naturally.

Leadership Development

With that understanding, the focus for the rest of this chapter will be on development of the leadership behaviors. The model we use for leadership development includes five steps. The graphic included here shows each of these steps.

Competency
Development
Assessed

Competency
Development

Competency
Development
Planning

Competencies
Assessed

Competencies
Determined

The first step is to determine the competencies. The competencies for The Character of Leadership are at the end of each chapter.

After the competencies are determined, the leader's existing proficiency in these competencies is assessed. This means, at minimum, a self-assessment, but ideally it also means gathering the ratings from others, who can give a full 360-degree view of the leader's competencies.

Armed with the knowledge of where the leader stands based on the leadership behaviors, the leader engages in a development plan. We advocate that these plans be in writing, contain specific activities the leader will engage in to build the competency, and that these plans be shared with others. Preferably they are shared with the people the leader is managing. Leadership development is a shared activity with one of the best tools being accountability to the team.

With the plan in place, the leader undertakes the activities of the development plan and once the plan is accomplished (usually one year), the leader is again assessed on the same competencies to determine the gain in proficiency.

Leadership Legacy

Making leadership development a priority will ensure that your leadership legacy is all you want it to be. Every person at his or her core is motivated to make a significant impact on people. This drive exists in all of us and takes many forms that can be accomplished in ways that have very little to do with leadership. But for the leader there is a unique and compelling reason to craft your legacy: At the end of your life, you will be able to look back with satisfaction at the lives you have touched positively and know without a doubt that your legacy will live on in the lives of those people.

Having a sense of your leadership legacy is important because this legacy does not depend on achieving your loftiest goals. You can have a powerful impact on others without ever seeing your own personal dreams become reality.

Alena always wanted to be a Broadway star. She was talented. She was a big hit in all her school programs. She received a great deal of encouragement from her teachers and her audiences. But as she moved deliberately toward her dream, life interfered. The death of her father and a faltering economy kept her from attending the performing arts school where she had been accepted. Instead, she enrolled in the local community college, received her teaching certificate, and took an entry-level position as a high school history teacher.

Alena faithfully taught her classes and participated in the school drama program, raising her own family at the same time. As she approached her fiftieth birthday, Alena saw the break she needed: Her kids were raised; her husband was mobile. She decided to leave the high school and pick up the pursuit of her Broadway dream. After all, her teaching career had merely been a holding cell where she incubated her dreams of the stage.

As she left her home on the morning she was to submit her resignation, her husband stopped her at the door. "You need to prepare yourself for the reaction your colleagues are going to have to your leaving," he told her. But Alena had never lost sight of her dream, had in fact considered her years as a teacher lost years. "They won't even know I am gone," she said.

Her husband shook his head. "I know you don't think you are important to those that you work with and to the students you have taught, but you don't see they way they look at you," he said. "I see how they look at you and believe me, they will be very sad that you are moving on." Alena shrugged, climbed into her car with a "whatever," and headed to school.

When she told the principal her decision she was surprised by his response. "Oh my!" he said, "What will we do? You're such an important part of our school. The kids are going to be so upset." Alena was even more surprised when he called an immediate meeting to have her tell the whole staff of her decision.

Her announcement at the meeting was met first with stunned silence, then tears. Finally, one person reluctantly congratulated her and then offered this tribute:

"Alena, you have been our rock. You defended us when the School Board wanted to make cuts in our programs. You encouraged us when the students were difficult. You mentored us when we were new; you challenged us when we were lazy; you cried with us when we hurt; and you collaborated with us when we were stuck. You are our leader and we will be lost without you."

Alena was stunned. She had never sought leadership; she was just passing time until her break came. What her husband had said was true, and the sense of loss for Alena was not rooted in leaving her colleagues or her students but rather in not realizing the enormous impact of her leadership along the way.

This is not a true story—or is it? If you are like Alena—and we all are in some way, realize the impact you have as a leader. See it now instead of at the end of your life. And with that recognition, build your leadership on a solid foundation of character. It may sound trite, but the reality is that you should develop your leadership because it is the right thing to do—for yourself and for those you lead and influence.

Bibliography

Collins, James C. Good to Great. New York, NY: HarperCollins Publishers, Inc., 2001.

Frankl, Viktor E. Man's Search for Meaning. Boston, MA: Beacon Press, 2006.

Good, Michael. The Search for Major Plagge: The Nazi Who Saved Jews. New York, NY: Fordham University Press, 2006.

Lansing, Alfred. Endurance: Shackleton's Incredible Voyage. New York, NY: Carroll & Graf Publishers, Inc., 1999.

Polanyi, Michael. Personal Knowledge: Towards a Post-Critical Philosophy. Chicago, IL: The University of Chicago Press, 1974.

Wheatley, Margaret J. Finding Our Way: Leadership For Uncertain Times. San Francisco, CA: Berrett-Koehler Publishers, Inc., 2005.

Web Resources:

"Joseph Stalin." Bio. Biography Channel. N.d. 25 Oct. 2008
<http://thebiographychannel.co.uk/biography_story/190:358/1/Josef_Stalin.htm

"Joseph Stalin Quotes." BrainyQuote. N.d. 13 Feb. 2009
<http://www.brainyquote.com/quotes/authors/j/joseph_stalin.html>

"Martin Luther King Speeches." MLKOnline. N.d. 29 Oct. 2008
< http://www.mlkonline.net/dream.html>

"Mohandas Gandhi." Bio. Biography Channel. N.d. 25 Oct. 2008.
<http://www.thebiographychannel.co.uk/biography_story/600:1125/1/Mohandas_Gandhi.htm>

"Mohandas Gandhi Quotes." BrainyQuote. N.d. 13 Feb. 2009.
<http://www.brainyquote.com/quotes/authors/m/mohandas_gandhi.html>

"Napoleon Bonaparte Quotes." BrainyQuote. N.d. 13 Feb. 2009.
<http://www.brainyquote.com/quotes/authors/n/napoleon_bonaparte.html>

"Viktor Frankl." Viktor Frankl Institut. N.d. 5 Jan. 2009.
<http:www.viktorfrankl.org./e/logotherapy.html>

"We Choose to Go to the Moon... ." The History Place/Great Speeches Collection. N.d. 17 Feb. 2009.
<http://www.historyplace.com/speeches/jfk-space.htm>

"Winston Churchill." Winston Churchill. N.d. 13 Feb. 2009.
<http://www.winstonchurchill.org/i4a/pages/index.cfm?pageid=418>